PARABLES
of a
TRAPPER

MARK BANDI MCDONALD

King James Version, public domain

Produced with the assistance of Fluency Organization, Inc

*To my wife, Marie, who always points me to
the Lord Jesus Christ.*

CONTENTS

ACKNOWLEDGMENTS

I want to thank my editor, Mary Ann Lackland and Fluency, who led me from rough draft handwritten stories to a finished book.

I also want to thank my friends who are trappers, fishermen, hunters, and outdoorsmen for their encouragement.

INTRODUCTION

I have been trapping wildlife since the age of seven. When I was a young boy, my father and his friends would take me hunting raccoons with hound dogs. On cold nights in the woods, sitting by the campfire under the stars, we would listen to the hound dogs trailing a raccoon as the men told me their hunting and trapping stories.

Many trappers like them had trapped mink, fox, and other fur-bearers to sustain their families and feed their children during the economic collapse of America's Great Depression when regular work was almost impossible to find. I learned many tricks of the trade listening to their stories about animal behavior, and I became a good trapper from a young age.

I am a richer man today because of the wealth of stories and wisdom they shared with me. Although many of those men are gone now, I will always have great admiration for backwoods country gentlemen who taught me well. I wrote this book to share with future generations what I've learned about animal behavior and life in the woods, along with some common sense application of Scripture that I hope you'll apply to your life.

Mark Bandi McDonald

Summer 2021

PARABLE OF TWO DOGS
THAT LOVED ME

During the winter of 1977-78 I trapped wolves, wolverine, lynx, fox, mink, and martin in the deep Alaskan wilderness. I lived alone, seventy miles from the nearest village, for ten months out of the year. My only company was two sled dogs that I used to pull firewood on a small sled. I dearly loved those two dogs, and I believe they held the same feelings for me.

My work consisted of running 142 steel traps and eighty snares. This line took me four days to run on snowshoes, fifteen miles a day, and required me to hike sixty miles in deep snow for the full trip. I ran each trap about twice a week.

Wolves at that time brought $350 per pelt, and I had various sets on popular trails, near moose carcasses, and in warm shelters to attract and trap the wolves. Before leaving my cabin for four days, I always locked my two dogs inside with plenty of food and water. If the dogs accompanied me, they would leave too much scent and scare away the fur-bearers I was trying to trap! Even worse, they might get caught in one of my traps.

After four days of hiking and camping in thirty to fifty below zero weather, I was cold and tired. I was looking forward to building a fire in a wood stove and resting in a real bed inside my log cabin base camp. As I neared home, I was terrified because I saw that the door was wide open and the dogs were gone. I feared they were both dead in a trap or snare on my trap line.

I turned around and ran my trail toward the first baited set that I'd intended for a wolverine. I could hear my dog Bunny howling long before I got there. She was weak, but alive. Bunny was a beautiful dog—half husky and half wolf—and weighed 108 pounds. To her credit, she had not fought the trap, even though her foot was badly damaged. The steel trap was too strong for her, and she knew only I could release her. So she had patiently waited for me.

I carried Bunny to the cabin to doctor her up. I was exhausted now, weak from my four-day hike and from carrying my 108-pound dog in my arms in the snow. My other dog Houche was still out there somewhere. However, I decided that if I tried to find Houche right then, I might die of hypothermia in the snowy wilderness. After I took care of Bunny, I ate and prepared to go to bed, praying that Houche would live until I could find her the next day.

That night with the wind howling, I heard the eerie scraping of a fir tree limb against the cabin walls just as I was falling asleep. So I thought it was my imagination when I also heard a faint scratching at my front door. I sprang up from my bed and threw open the door. There was Houche—my beautiful Norwegian Elkhound—in perfect health except for being hungry!

Houche had trailed me sixty miles, bypassing 142 traps and eighty snares—passing delicious bait while hungry, passing wolf urine on bushes without pausing to smell it, ignoring curiosity lures, passing warm dens and shelters to get out of the cold, walking right by my campfire ashes, and looking the other way when she saw my traps on moose carcasses. Therefore, she never got caught!

How could this be? Was it a miracle? What was the dog's secret? I knew I would soon find out how she did it, but for now I was just thankful Houche was alive. We all three slept a hard sleep in the warm cabin all night.

The next week I ran the trap line where Houche had somehow avoided all my traps. Not many animals had moved around that week. Any track that I saw in the snow led straight to one of my traps, but I did not see any of Houche's tracks leading to a trap.

She had learned an important trick to avoid the snares. I saw her tracks only in the center of my snowshoe tracks! Houche did not look to the left or right, no matter how cold she got, no matter how hungry she got, and no matter how curious she was. Even when she was bone-tired, she would not seek shelter because she was focused on my tracks leading her home.

One thing drove Houche—she desperately desired to be with me and followed my snowshoe tracks until she found me! She knew that if she found me, I would feed her, give her shelter, and love her. Houche and Bunny made it home safely because they were two dogs who loved me—and they knew I loved them too.

Horse-Sense Interpretation

The two dogs in this story represent two people trying to reach God and find Him. One gets caught in a trap like Bunny, distracted by his own wants, needs, or desires. That person, however, is at least smart enough to know he is not strong enough to escape the trap on his own. Instead of wasting strength and energy fighting a battle he cannot win, he calls out for help and waits. Only God has the ability and the desire to set him free and heal his wounds. Therefore, minimal damage occurs because he realizes his limitations and calls on an unlimited God!

The principle here is the importance of waiting on God when we find ourselves in trouble. He will rescue us. We may be in pain while we wait, but God will find us and take care of us.

The other person is more like Houche in this story. He is able to walk in very dangerous territory and not get caught because he puts his needs and wants aside. This wise person decides to follow hard after God, knowing that when he finds God, He will provide for all his needs and love him. The harder we follow after God, the safer we will be. If we have a passion to follow God's Word exactly—and follow him very closely—we are less likely to fall into a trap.

> *And now, Israel, what doth the Lord thy God require of thee, but to fear the Lord thy God, to walk in all his ways, and to love him, and to serve the Lord thy God with all thy heart and with all thy soul.*
> **Deuteronomy 10:12**

> *And he said to them all, "If any man will come after me, let him deny himself, and take up his cross daily, and follow me."*
> **Luke 9:23**

The righteous cry, and the Lord heareth, and delivereth them out of all their troubles. The Lord is nigh unto them that are of a broken heart; and saveth such as be of a contrite spirit. Many are the afflictions of the righteous: but the Lord delivereth him out of them all.

Psalm 34:17-19

Blessed is the man that endureth temptation: for when he is tried, he shall receive the crown of life, which the Lord hath promised to them that love him.

James 1:12

He healeth the broken in heart, and bindeth up their wounds.

Psalm 147:3

But seek ye first the kingdom of God, and his righteousness; and all these things shall be added unto you.

Matthew 6:33

I cried unto the Lord with my voice; with my voice unto the Lord did I make my supplication. I poured out my complaint before him; I shewed before him my trouble.

Psalm 142:1-2

Even so it is not the will of your Father which is in heaven, that one of these little ones should perish.
Matthew 18:14

My soul followeth hard after thee: thy right hand upholdeth me.
Psalm 63:8

And ye shall seek me, and find me, when ye shall search for me with all your heart.
Jeremiah 29:13

The Spirit of the Lord God is upon me; because the Lord hath anointed me to preach good tidings unto the meek; he hath sent me to bind up the brokenhearted, to proclaim liberty to the captives, and the opening of the prison to them that are bound.
Isaiah 61:1

If the Son therefore shall make you free, ye shall be free indeed.
John 8:36

PARABLE OF THE
TEXAS HORNY TOAD

I love horny toads. They are round, flat lizards that look like miniature dinosaurs and are ten times as wide and fat as a lizard. They eat ants with their sticky, frog-like tongue and are harmless to humans. Who wouldn't love a horny toad?

The interesting thing about horny toads is that they can run but cannot climb because of their shape and their short, stubby legs. They're unable to wiggle their body like a snake, and their limbs curve out, instead of inward like a lizard's. They can use them to flip sand on their backs or cover themselves with dirt, but they cannot climb. Unlike lizards you see climbing walls around your house, a horny toad's limbs also lack suction cups. If they fall into a cup just three inches deep, they cannot get themselves out.

Horny toads are becoming scarce in Texas and are protected by the government. In fact, it is illegal to possess or trap them. However, I accidentally caught four of them one time when I was digging post holes while building a fence in Ben Wheeler, Texas. It was hot that day, and I took a break to get a cold drink at a nearby convenience store. I met someone at the store and spent the rest of the day doing another job for them. I ended up leaving the post holes open for two days. When I returned, I saw three horny toads in one post hole and one more in another post hole.

Very carefully, I reached in to pick them up and release them. As I set the fence posts the rest of the day, I thought about how sad it was that the horny toads could not save themselves. If I hadn't come along, they would have died. That being said, if the horny toads had been more careful, they wouldn't have gotten into a situation they were not designed to get out of.

For all its limitations, the horny toad is also very gifted. It can do things very few other animals are designed to do. For example, if the weather turns very cold or food is scarce, the horny toad can go into a hibernation-like state for up to three years. It doesn't require water to survive and, in fact, can live without water its entire lifetime because it gets all the water it needs from its diet of ants.

The horny toad and red ant have a special symbiotic relationship, too. They need each other to exist. The horny toad's digestive system runs on a certain acid that is only produced by one ant in the world—you guessed it, the red ant! The horny toad is a roadrunner's favorite food, but it can hide by flipping dirt on top of itself until it is perfectly camouflaged. If the ground temperature is 150 degrees in the desert, a horny toad can dig down where it's a cool 80-90 degrees to seek shelter. God gave the horny toad some unique abilities we don't see repeated in all of creation.

Horse-Sense Interpretation

Albert Einstein once said, "The difference between a genius and a fool is the genius knows his limitations." Everyone has gifts and limitations. It is important not to attempt what you are not qualified to do, because of your natural limitations. You have special gifts, but you cannot do everything. You and I are limited. We can't be someone we are not. We can do so much for the Lord, but we are still limited. The best strategy is to be like the horny toad and find what you are good at doing and give God the credit for giving you that gift.

For example, I'm weak in chemistry and math and barely got through trigonometry and algebra in school. But I always had a natural curiosity about the world and animals, so biology came easily to me. I've been able to build a diverse career around my love for nature. Like the horny toad, we should stick to what we are good at and back away from situations that point out our weaknesses. It's so easy to fall into a hole in life and not be able to get ourselves out of it!

Iron sharpeneth iron; so a man sharpeneth the countenance of his friend.

Proverbs 27:17

Every man shall give as he is able, according to the blessing of the Lord thy God which he hath given thee.

Deuteronomy 16:17

Whoso boasteth himself of a false gift is like clouds and wind without rain.

Proverbs 25:14

For I say, through the grace given unto me, to every man that is among you, not to think of himself more highly than he ought to think; but to think soberly, according as God hath dealt to every man the measure of faith.

Romans 12:3

PARABLE OF
TRAPPING WILD HOGS

The wild hogs in East Texas where I live destroy millions of dollars of agricultural products every year. After a herd of wild pigs takes over a coastal meadow, it looks like a drunk driver on a tractor with a breaking plow has been wandering all night in the fields. The hogs ruin all the rare plants, damage the wildlife habitat, and spread diseases to healthy livestock and wildlife. They also pollute the waterways with E-coli and various other parasites and bacteria. They are like living vacuum cleaners, eating all the acorns and hickory nuts they can find—starving out the native wildlife.

The large boars are so raunchy and taste so disgusting that even the buzzards rarely visit a carcass. Some people consider the sows and pigs fit to eat, but they cook the meat very, very well-done to prevent disease and parasites from getting into their system. Several golf courses, ranches, and farms have hired me over the years to shoot, trap, and snare wild hogs on their property. But it's not easy work.

At first, I typically use a large cage trap to catch a few. Then they get wise! At that point, I can only hunt the remaining hogs at night and snare them with black bear snares. I learned from the Fish and Wildlife agency how to build a large pen and freely feed the hogs visiting inside it for a week or two before setting the trap door. This clever design catches many hogs. The only problem is that the intelligence of a wild hog is surprisingly high and they figure out my plan. The smartest animals in the world are man, followed by dolphins, chimpanzees, and then wild hogs. I'm not sure sometimes if that order isn't actually in reverse because these hogs are so extremely difficult to catch!

One rancher told me a story about catching 120 hogs in two months using a large circle trap. However, a herd of 20 or so remained outside of his grasp. They were all followers of a stunted, ugly 150-pound boar with one tusk broken off. Most of these pigs were inbred. They were small and either black or red in color. Their leader protected them by wisely keeping them out of the rancher's hay meadow, away from his traps, and outside of firing range. Frustrated, the rancher asked if I could help catch them.

It was going to be a tough job, so I told him I would have to think about it before giving him my answer. I thought a few days then consulted with a hog farmer. He said he had a registered black and white show boar that he could use to trap those remaining 20 hogs.

"How can you do that?" I wanted to know.

"I've caught hundreds of wild hogs with this show boar," he explained. "See, he is the Boss Hog on my place. All the other hogs either follow him, serve him, or he kills and eats them. Boss Hog has a lot of followers that way."

The farmer went on to explain that this boar could call to the other hogs, talk to them, and control them. "Pigs love him, Mark. He's good-looking, slick-talking, and a natural leader."

That description made me think of a politician or two, but I said nothing. The farmer told me he planned to use his prize boar and feed him in a large pen trap on the rancher's property for a few days to get him used to his surroundings. Then he would turn the boar loose to attract the wild herd.

"They will follow Boss Hog," he assured me. "And he will either drive off or kill that ugly stunted boar. No one will be left then to protect them, so they'll just follow Boss Hog instead. When they follow him into the trap I set, we will slaughter them—except for Boss Hog, of course. I need him!"

I put the rancher and this wise hog farmer together to work on the job—and I walked away since I wasn't needed.

Soon the rancher called me with an update. "Mark, I can't believe it! That pretty black and white boar led every hog into that trap exactly like that farmer said would happen.

And that ugly stunted boar? He disappeared from the county!"

Then the rancher asked, "What do I owe you for lining me up with that hog farmer and his good-looking boar?"

I smiled and answered, "Just tell your friends to be careful how they vote and who they follow."

Horse-Sense Interpretation

Who is your Boss Hog? Like the boars in this story, we have to be careful. The people we follow—politicians, teachers, leaders, pastors—have a lot of influence on us. Someone whose heart and intentions are wrong may look good on the outside, but they may be leading us straight into a trap.

Whenever the religious system and political system of a society have intertwined in history, the enslavement of the people followed. I call them leaders with a "Herodian spirit" after the evil King Herod in the Bible who catered to Rome—and the Jewish religious leaders—telling them whatever they wanted to hear. Half-religious and half-politician leaders are especially dangerous. They attract us by what they say and do, and we can let them lead us into dangerous territory because we depend on them to protect us and provide for us. Pick your leaders carefully. Do your homework and research the issues at stake. Above all, follow Jesus.

> *Woe unto them that decree unrighteous decrees, and that write grievousness which they have prescribed; To turn aside the needy from judgment, and to take away the right from the poor of my people, that widows may be their prey, and that they may rob the fatherless!*
> **Isaiah 10:1-2**

> *That the hypocrite reign not, lest the people be ensnared.*
> **Job 34:30**

> *It is not good to accept the person of the wicked, to overthrow the righteous in judgment.*
> **Proverbs 18:5**

> *A prudent man foreseeth the evil, and hideth himself; but the simple pass on, and are punished.*
> **Proverbs 27:12**

> *When the righteous are in authority, the people rejoice: but when the wicked beareth rule, the people mourn.*
> **Proverbs 29:2**

> *My sheep hear my voice, and I know them, and they follow me.*
> **John 10:27**

> *Fools make a mock at sin: but among the righteous there is favour.*
> **Proverbs 14:9**

Parable of the Innocent Rabbit and Squirrel

A snowshoe hare is a big, fluffy, white rabbit. In the winter these rabbits are hard to spot because their fur matches the snow. They are light-footed for their size and gently make their way through the snow as they hunt for food. Under normal circumstances, they do not step with enough force to trigger a foot trap as they innocently follow their trails in the North Country, also known as Alaska.

I had three friends in a town called Manley Hot Springs, Alaska—Mike, Cathy, and Paula. Knowing the difficulties of catching snowshoe hares with a foot trap, Cathy taught me one day how to snare them instead with picture-hanging wire. She used a two-foot section of wire and tied a four-inch slipknot. Then she hung these slip knots at ninety-degree angles above a rabbit trail, about three inches off the ground. When the rabbit innocently made its way down this trail (like it had done many times before) it would get caught in the snare.

Cathy told me that squirrels get in trouble the same way, innocently playing on logs all day—running, sitting, and eating on top of them. "A squirrel feels at home on a log and plays innocently at these locations," Cathy explained.

The Choctaw Indians in Oklahoma take advantage of a squirrel's innocence by creating a trap from two logs and a figure-four notched stick used for a trigger. They place the two logs on top of each other with four guideposts on each side. One end of the log is raised about eighteen inches off the bottom log with the notched trigger stick baited with a pecan. Without thinking, the playful, innocent squirrel reaches for the pecan and the top log falls on him.

Horse-Sense Interpretation

You don't have to be guilty to find yourself caught in a trap. In other words, the rabbit and squirrel aren't doing anything wrong—running trails and playing on logs. But they get caught in a trap! There are traps set for the innocent everywhere these days. Jesus alone can set you free.

For example, it's not a sin to be broke—but financial difficulty is a trap. It's not a sin to be rejected, but depending so much on others to meet your needs is a trap. Marijuana may be legal in some states, but it can still ensnare you with an addiction that you can't escape from. Stay close to Jesus, and He will keep you from being ensnared by people and situations that can harm you.

> *The thief cometh not, but for to steal, and to kill, and to destroy: I am come that they might have life, and that they might have it more abundantly.*
>
> **John 10:10**

> *Looking unto Jesus the author and finisher of our faith; who for the joy that was set before him endured the cross, despising the shame, and is set down at the right hand of the throne of God. For consider him that endured such contradiction of sinners against himself, lest ye be wearied and faint in your minds.*
>
> **Hebrews 12:2-3**

> *The wicked have laid a snare for me: yet I erred not from thy precepts.*
>
> **Psalm 119:110**

> *My son, if sinners entice thee, consent thou not. If they say, Come with us, let us lay wait for blood, let us lurk privily for the innocent without cause.*
>
> **Proverbs 1:10-11**

PARABLE OF
CAPTURING WILD HORSES

All my life, I dreamed of catching wild horses. I wanted to run them down on a good cow horse working alongside a bunch of good cowboys. My favorite dream involved herding a wild remuda into a corral—a ranch hand term for a herd of horses. And then I would rope the best one and ride it until it couldn't buck anymore.

However, growing up in the big city of Dallas, Texas, in the late 1970s and 'coon hunting in the hardwood river bottoms of East Texas did not allow me much of a chance to pursue that dream. So instead, I settled for riding saddle broncs and bulls in rodeos and listening to tales from real Western cowboy about their adventures capturing wild horses.

One cowboy I met was a purebred registered Apache Indian. He asked me not to use his name in this book, so I'll call him Running Water to hide his identity. Running Water

33

told me about his many adventures chasing wild horses on the Reservation and acres of land owned by the government. He and half a dozen young Indians spent many years herding and roping wild horses in the Desert Mountains near the Reservation. He told of broken arms and legs, horse bites, and bruises. But to me, it all sounded like fun to be a cowboy!

Running Water had an unusual connection with nature and was one of the best trainers I've ever met. He could train a wild horse to kneel down to the ground in order for a handicap person to be able to pet him. My friend could also put a chicken to sleep for hours just by swinging it around and then tucking one foot under one wing and its head under another, a trick his dad had taught him. We could leave and come back four hours later and find the chicken still sleeping!

Running Water once roped a horse in deep snow, but before he could dally the rope around the saddle horn (to secure the horse and protect his hands and fingers from the rope), the wild horse pulled him out of the saddle! Like any good cowboy, Running Water refused to let go of the lariat —the rope cowboys use for lassoing.

That wild horse outran Running Water's companions for over a mile until another Indian's quick lasso and stout horse finally stopped it. Running Water was still holding onto the rope! Thankfully by this time, the wild horse was out of fight. It let the other Indians lead it back to the Reservation, this time with Running Water on its back. He was exhausted with broken ribs, bruises, cuts, and—according to his friends—a big smile on his face the whole way home.

I was young and so was Running Water when I first heard these stories. Running Water told me he broke about 10 horses a year at that time. His buddies sold the horses they would catch in order to buy groceries and beer. I looked him up later when I was in my fifties to check on him. When we talked, I asked him if he still caught wild horses. I wanted to know how he was holding up physically, since we are about the same age.

He laughed and said, "I can catch and train wild horses better now than when I was young!"

That sounded amazing. How could that be true? I wanted to know more about how he lured the horses, so I asked if he built a trap or something. I also assumed there were others helping him.

To my surprise, he told me, "A friend goes out and catches the horses by himself and brings them to me."

I had to find out how that worked, so I made plans to drive to his forty-acre ranch adjourning millions of acres of government-owned wilderness and Reservation land. On his ranch were ten of the nicest wild mountain horses I have ever seen. There was one beautiful stud among the herd, and when Running Water whistled, the stud came running to him.

Watching the two, it was obvious that the horse loved Running Water and obeyed his every word.

"I raised this stud on goat milk," my friend told me. "I slept with it, talked to it, and have trained it ever since a lightning strike killed its mother."

He continued, "See, he is now the strongest, fastest horse in this country. Him and me are partners on this ranch."

Then Running Water pointed to the horse's feet. "Look at his feet," he told me. I did so. "Come on, pick 'em up and look!" he encouraged me. "I made him special horseshoes that won't slip on wet mountain rock."

I was shocked. "You mean to tell me that at your age you are still running down and roping wild horses on those steep, slick mountains?"

He shook his head, pointed to his cabin nearby, and smiled. "No! I watch television, drink, eat, and rest while my horse goes alone to catch the wild horses for me."

I doubted that. "Well, how do you do that?" I asked.

He replied simply, "I open the gate."

Now I was really confused. Sarcastically, I said, "Oh, so that stud just goes out, catches horses, and brings them home to you, huh? I don't see why he'd come back!"

Running Water answered, "He comes back because he loves me and I feed him."

"But aren't you afraid that some wild stallion will kill him?"

At this, Running Water just laughed and replied, "If there is a fight, remember he has special shoes and won't slip. When he kicks, it's like fighting a boxer wearing brass knuckles!"

Horse-Sense Interpretation

Like Running Water, God is looking out for the orphan, the stranger, the fatherless and the motherless to love, feed, and care for. He will take the weak and rejected in society and make them strong because they are so deeply loved.

When a person like that knows the love and provision of God, they will bring others into the fold just like that horse did for my friend. I've seen it happen over and over in my lifetime. Someone the world has rejected becomes someone God can use. He becomes a strong witness for God among a crowd of people very few people could reach.

Like Running Water equipping his horse with those special shoes, God also protects and equips his witnesses so that they can be a light for him, even among a very rough crowd like the wild mountain horses. Unbelievers will hear what these witnesses have to say about Jesus, and they listen to them and respect them because they have a shared experience. Many unbelievers decide to accept God's love and start a new life this way. And their lives change forever!

When my father and my mother forsake me, then the Lord will take me up.
Psalm 27:10

The Lord is nigh unto them that are of a broken heart; and saveth such as be of a contrite spirit.
Psalm 34:18

Finally, my brethren, be strong in the Lord, and in the power of his might. And your feet shod with the preparation of the gospel of peace;
Ephesians 6:10, 15

And he said unto me, "MY GRACE IS SUFFICIENT FOR THEE, FOR MY STRENGTH IS MADE PERFECT IN WEAKNESS." Most gladly therefore will I rather glory in my infirmities, that the power of Christ may rest upon me.
2 Corinthians 12:9

PARABLE OF THE FREELOADING FLYING SQUIRREL

The flying squirrel lives in hollow trees, bird nesting boxes, and the leaf nests made by fox squirrels. They have a special weakness for bird feeders and often raid them at night in search of food. Most squirrel-proof birdfeeders are ineffective at preventing flying squirrels from their nighttime raids because these little creatures don't climb up to the feeders. They softly glide down to them!

In fact, if you place a bluebird or wren nesting box close to a large oak, pecan, or hickory tree about 10 feet high on the trunk—and then place a bird feeder nearby—you have created the perfect spot for a flying squirrel to call home. Instead of the birds you hoped to attract, the flying squirrel will promptly move into the bird nesting box. They freeload on the homeowner who put up the bird nest box, not to mention taking away from the birds who may have already built a nice, comfy nest inside. These squirrels take advantage of the situation for their own benefit.

Most homeowners who are bird lovers would rather have beautiful birds over flying squirrels. To catch these squirrels, I have a certain technique. I simply go to the bird nesting box, place a pillowcase over the opening, and knock on the birdhouse. These freeloading flying squirrels panic, run into the pillowcase, and I take them away. It works every time!

Horse-Sense Interpretation

Do not freeload on people. You shouldn't steal others' food or stay in someone else's house free of charge. Instead, work until you can own or rent your own place.

Many adult children fall into a bad habit of freeloading off their parents, much like the freeloading flying squirrel. They have learned that it's easier to take advantage of a situation than to go out and find work to support themselves.

There are exceptions. Sometimes we must rely on others to help us for a season—that's a different situation. If you are living with family or friends, pay your part of the bills and work around the house to help them out until you can get on your feet. But a freeloader is a con-artist. There is an honorable way to rely on someone's help temporarily—and there is a dishonorable, selfish way that takes advantage of someone's good nature.

"My parents have enough money. Why should I have to work?" I've heard adult children say many times. The biblical model is that of several generations living together, but they all supported each other in good and bad times. Parents took care of the kids, and the kids took care of the parents in their old age.

Even in nature it works like that. When a beaver kid is two-and-a-half years old, the papa beaver runs them out to be on their own. The young beaver doesn't like being independent at first, but he eventually builds a home of his own and starts a family. However, if the papa beaver is killed in a fight or trapped, the kids all stay with the mother in the family den and care for her the rest of her life.

The freeloading flying squirrel just cheats other animals out of their homes. Someone who lives like that among family and friends needs to repent and start building a life of his own. I work in a jail ministry, and that's the advice I give men when they are released from prison. Because they often live with someone at first to make ends meet, I tell them to rake the yard, do the dishes, and pay their own way to demonstrate that they want to help the people who are helping them.

If a person tells me they still can't find work after a while, I have the same advice. I always say, "If you can't find a job, offer to work for free." If you will work for free, God will honor you and soon give you money-making work.

There is a growing mentality in America that says, "You owe me!" No one owes you anything! If you stay busy, you will not get depressed by your circumstances. Eventually, things will turn around for you! Just ask the beaver!

> *Withdraw thy foot from thy neighbour's house; lest he be weary of thee, and so hate thee.*
> **Proverbs 25:17**

> *The ants are a people not strong, yet they prepare their meat in the summer; The conies are but a feeble folk, yet make they their houses in the rocks.*
> **Proverbs 30:25-26**

> *Neither did we eat any man's bread for nought; but wrought with labour and travail night and day, that we might not be chargeable to any of you:*
> **2 Thessalonians 3:8**

> *For even when we were with you, this we commanded you, that if any would not work, neither should he eat.*
> **2 Thessalonians 3:10**

Parable of Good Friends, Bad Advice, and an Acrobatic Skunk

Good friends are rare and very valuable. Good advice is even more rare, but it is difficult to mine the good advice out of the scrap piles lining the information highway. This parable is about how an acrobatic skunk educated me on the difference between good friends and good advice. I learned that the two do not always walk alongside one another.

When I was young, I trapped a few skunks by accident while hunting grey fox and coyotes. I would shoot and skin the skunks, and they brought in anywhere from two to five dollars for each one. It became inconvenient to kill and skin the skunks when I began college, however. My classmates also seemed to be annoyed by my extra-curricular activity. In order to respect them, I fasted from skinning the skunks. I just shot the skunks and left them. This strategy put a trap or two out of commission until either the owls or buzzards would clean the skunk carcass.

I needed all my traps in working order in order to make a living, so I discussed my skunk problem with a professor at my college who had a Ph.D. in Wildlife and two great friends, Mark Couch and Cody Livingston.

Mark and Cody knew I felt wasteful for killing and not skinning the skunks, so they counselled me to release them instead. They regularly caught skunks and claimed to have a secret technique to turn them loose without getting sprayed. These good friends of mine described in detail their technique for safely releasing a skunk from a steel trap.

The technique involved a series of steps, starting with talking softly to the trapped skunk. They said I should walk up to the set slowly and then quickly lay a long pole over the skunk's tail and head. Firmly holding down the tail, I should then put my foot on the trap's spring to release the skunk and back away slowly. Cody and Mark said it was impossible for a skunk to spray, as long as his tail and hind legs were held down.

Something seemed strange about their exuberant joy and confidence in telling me about this "skunk secret." I decided I needed to seek a more professional opinion, which led me to talk to my college teacher about it. He had trapped as a graduate student, so I asked him one day, "If you hold down a skunk's back feet and tail, can he spray?"

My teacher confidently replied, "Mark, it is biologically impossible for a skunk to spray, if both feet are on the ground and his tail is held down."

Armed with advice from my two great friends and one brilliant college professor, how could I go wrong? I was ready to apply the technique for myself. Mark accompanied me in order to coach me along as I made my first attempt to release a skunk and not get sprayed. As we approached the trapped skunk, Mark handed me two four-foot-long poles and started backing up in the opposite direction.

I said, "Hey, I thought you were going to teach me how to do this?"

He smiled and answered from afar, "Calm down! I'll teach you...just do exactly what I say."

I said, "Wait a minute. Why don't you just do it for me and show me how?"

He shook his head and said, "I already know how—you're the one who needs to learn. You need to do it yourself." Mark continued coaching me along, telling me to continue walking slowly toward the skunk.

I did that and thought, "So far, so good."

"Now, kneel down slowly and put one pole over his tail," Mark told me.

I put the pole over the skunk's tail, holding it down firmly. Nothing happened. "It's working!" I bragged. "What do I do now?"

"Use your left hand and put the other pole behind the skunk's head and hold it steady."

I did what I was told. "He's helpless now. It works! What do I do next?"

Mark then started laughing and backed even farther in the opposite direction. Meanwhile, I kept holding down the skunk's back feet and head. Then something happened that's hard to describe. It's difficult to imagine that it is even biologically possible, but the skunk poked both barrels of scent glands to the side of its tail, and green liquid gas came straight at me, full force!

That potent smell was strong enough to blind me. I rolled down the hill to the creek and held my head underwater, eyes open, trying to clear the acid out of them.

Despite saving my sight, my eyes, nose, and throat continued to burn. I shouted to my "good" friend, "You lied to me! You set me up and I trusted you!"

At this point, he was rolling on the ground with laughter. "You didn't follow the instructions I gave you," he cried. "You messed up, and now look at what you've done to yourself! You can't even turn a skunk loose. Some trapper you are! I can do it anytime I want to. You don't even know how to follow instructions. So don't be mad at me when it's your fault!"

To this day, a professor and two good friends still say I did something wrong, since they claim a skunk can't spray with his tail down.

But I know an acrobatic skunk that can!

Horse-Sense Interpretation

This parable is about people who come across as holier-than thou. They are always eager to give you advice, but they may not follow their own rules.

I received some sorry counsel from some people I trusted. But I had never seen them demonstrate what they were telling me to do. If someone gives you advice about how to live and be successful, see if they consistently demonstrate that advice in their own lives. Or else you may get "skunked"!

See if the person giving you advice has lived it; ask them to show you an example of how they practice what they preach; and check to see if the love of God is clearly present in their advice. Or are they just telling you what to do?

A friend can lead you astray. A friend can be a good friend, but lack wisdom. Not every good friend gives good advice.

You must follow someone who shows you the love of God and who also wants the best for you. It's up to you to do your homework before following their counsel. I learned the hard way that bad advice stinks!

Which say, Stand by thyself, come not near to me; for I am holier than thou. These are a smoke in my nose, a fire that burneth all the day.
Isaiah 65:5

The fear of the Lord is the instruction of wisdom; and before honour is humility.
Proverbs 15:33

Understanding is a wellspring of life unto him that hath it: but the instruction of fools is folly.
Proverbs 16:22

Hear counsel, and receive instruction, that thou mayest be wise in thy latter end. There are many devices in a man's heart; nevertheless the counsel of the Lord, that shall stand.
Proverbs 19:20-21

For I have given you an example, that ye should do as I have done to you.
John 13:15

Let no man despise thy youth; but be thou an example of the believers, in word, in conversation, in charity, in spirit, in faith, in purity.

1 Timothy 4:12

Be ye therefore followers of God, as dear children; And walk in love, as Christ also hath loved us, and hath given himself for us an offering and a sacrifice to God for a sweetsmelling savour.

Ephesians 5:1-2

PARABLE OF THE
"BIG, BAD BULL ELK"

I once did some work at a subdivision created out of a 2,600-acre high-fenced exotic game ranch in Athens, Texas. The developer hired me to perform some wildlife consulting and trapping. The selling point of this new subdivision was that residents could walk and drive the roads while viewing wild unusual animals like zebra, axis-deer, fallow deer, sika deer, black buck antelope, white tail deer, elk, and other native wildlife. It sounds like a Walt Disney Bambi movie, but in reality, elk are very dangerous when the autumn rutting season comes around.

I suggested to the developer that we capture the elk and move them to a safe 60-acre pen to prevent humans from being attacked by these animals that are unpredictable and violent in the mating season, always looking for a fight. The bull elk were full grown elk—marvelous animals weighing 600 to 1,000 pounds with huge 7x7 and even 7x8 racks of deadly antlers.

To rope these elk would be dangerous to cowboys and their horses, and to trap them would cause injury to the elk. So I had to come up with an alternative. I determined there was only one logical way to capture these big, bad bull elk. Drugs! I used a tranquilizer gun and shot the elk with drugs to sedate them. If I gave one .01cc too much of the drug, it would kill the elk. If I gave an elk .01cc too little of the drug, he might kill me.

On the first day, I loaded the gun with .6cc of sucostrim and shot the first elk in the rear end. In three minutes, this big, bad bull elk was down on the ground helpless. The elk could still see me and hear me, but he was totally powerless because the drug paralyzed his muscles for a short time.

Under the influence of drugs, it took only a few minutes for four men and myself to carry this dangerous animal like a sleeping baby to the transport trailer. We repeated this process with each elk and safely moved them where we wanted them. The elk were helpless to do anything about it, and we were all kept safe.

Horse-Sense Interpretation

When you are drunk or under the influence of drugs, you can be maneuvered, carried off, and manipulated by anyone or any spiritual power forces, such as demons under the control of Satan. The bull elk in this parable was ten times stronger than a man—except when it was under the influence of drugs. One-tenth of a teaspoon was all it took to render him helpless.

I've also seen blackbirds eat poisonous china berries until they died, but they couldn't stop eating them because they tasted good. I once saw a fat and drunk raccoon in a daze sitting on the side of the road in Austin after having eaten too many overripe blackberries. He was an easy target for a car to come by and run him over.

Drugs and alcohol lower your defenses. Does anyone really want to be controlled or manipulated by evil forces? Don't put yourself in control of powers that you are powerless to overcome.

"But it's legal," some would say. Did you know that prescription drug abuse is the number one problem in drug abuse in America? Abusing any kind of drug can make you an easy target for Satan. He comes to kill, steal, and destroy, according to the Bible. Don't let that happen to you.

Wine is a mocker, strong drink is raging: and whosoever is deceived thereby is not wise.
Proverbs 20:1

Who hath woe? who hath sorrow? who hath contentions? who hath babbling? who hath wounds without cause? who hath redness of eyes? They that tarry long at the wine; they that go to seek mixed wine. At the last it biteth like a serpent, and stingeth like an adder. Thine eyes shall behold strange women, and thine heart shall utter perverse things. Yea, thou shalt be as he that lieth down in the midst of the sea, or as he that lieth upon the top of a mast. They have stricken me, shalt thou say, and I was not sick; they have beaten me, and I felt it not: when shall I awake? I will seek it yet again.
Proverbs 23:29-30, 32-35

Forsake the foolish, and live; and go in the way of understanding.
Proverbs 9:6

There hath no temptation taken you but such as is common to man: but God is faithful, who will not suffer you to be tempted above that ye are able; but will with the temptation also make a way to escape, that ye may be able to bear it.
1 Corinthians 10:13

PARABLE OF BEING CAUGHT IN MY OWN TRAP

When I was a young boy, I found a catfish living inside a Coke can in a creek and wondered how it got there. The catfish was far too large to have come inside the can through the drinking hole. I finally figured out what happened. The catfish went into the can when it was small and kept eating anything else that happened to wander inside the can until he was too big and fat to escape!

That catfish originally went in the can to hide and catch some food, but it was not smart enough to realize that he was trapping himself! I remember thinking back then as a kid, "How can anyone be stupid enough to trap himself in his own set?" Little did I know that it would happen to me one day.

Beaver pelts brought a high price in the winter of 1977 in Alaska where I was working as a trapper. "Work" was the term they used instead of "trapping" in those days, whenever you said the word, "beaver." Each lake near my trapping territory had a beaver hut, and within a few hundred feet of their hut was an underwater pile of limbs the beavers stored for eating in the winter. Several underwater trails ran between the hut and feed piles.

To trap the beaver, I had to set a trap between the hut and the food cache. In order to set a trap in the underwater trail, I had to chop a two- to four-foot-wide hole in the ice covering the frozen lake. I used a deadly trap called a conibear trap that crushes a beaver instantly. The trap is a square pattern of jaws with two strong springs. I used a special tool to set the conibear trap or to get a dead beaver out of one.

One day I was setting a trap for a beaver on a trail in water ten feet deep. To make this set, I used a three-inch poplar tree pole that was fifteen feet long. I wore big six-foot-long snowshoes because the snow was soft and deep on top of the lake. As I was pushing the trap pole through the hole in the ice, I slipped. Before I knew it, both of my hands hit the trap's trigger! And to make it worse, I fell headfirst with the pole into the icy water.

I could not swim since both of my arms were hopelessly caught in the unforgiving trap, not to mention my heavy clothing and snowshoes weighing me down. Fighting for my life, I held my breath and maneuvered one end of the pole to rest on the bottom of the lakebed and pushed myself out of the water onto the snow. I was alive, but I was trapped and alone in twenty-five-degree below zero weather, two miles away from my cabin.

I remembered some advice I'd received from two teenage Athabaskan Indians in the summer. They told me that if you fall into ice water, in the wilderness, in Alaska, in winter...if you are real fast, you can shoot yourself before you freeze to death! I didn't like that advice. However, earlier in the fall, an old Indian taught me a trick that did end up saving my life.

He told me to always wear layers of wool clothing in case I ever fell into icy water. The outside layer, he explained, will freeze, and the other layers of clothes will remain wet but unfrozen. He then said if God was with me, and I was tough enough, it would be possible to make it to camp and survive. Thank God I'd taken his advice and worn layers of wool that morning.

Carrying the steel trap and poplar tree pole with my trapped arms, I somehow eventually made it to my cabin. By then, my hands were frozen stiff, along with the rest of my body. My beard was frozen to my coat, and my toboggan was frozen to my hair. I was also minus one snowshoe.

I was home, but there was still one major problem. I could not go through the cabin doorway because the pole that the trap and I were hooked to was fifteen feet long! I had only one choice. Praying that I wouldn't snap my frozen arms in two, I rammed the door down with the pole. Exhausted, I went inside and stood over my barrel stove as I slowly thawed.

I screamed in pain from the frostbite, the kind of pain that is equal to anything a fire can cause. I've often wondered if God could use cold for hell instead of heat. It's that bad! The more my beard melted, the more it freed my mouth to scream. I guess every animal within thirty miles heard me yelling, but there were no people to hear my cries for help.

I was warmer now, but my arms were still trapped. I continued praying, and God gave me an idea. I could use my mouth to weave a rope slowly through the trap springs, one at a time.

So I carefully tied a slipknot with my mouth on the end of a rope. I then carefully put the slipknot on my mukluks (boots) and flipped onto my back so that I could hold the other end of the rope in my teeth. I pulled with my teeth and held pressure on the springs until they released. After three hours of sheer misery, I escaped from my own trap. That makes me a lot more blessed and a little smarter than a catfish!

Horse-Sense Interpretation

When you try to deceive, trap, or manipulate other people, you can end up in the trap yourself, with no one to help you out. Traps come in all shapes and sizes today. For example, we tell one little lie, and then it takes another lie to hide from the first lie. Pretty soon, our lives are full of lies, and we can't get out of the trap of our own making.

Have you ever opened your mouth to speak when you shouldn't? That's a trap!

Have you ever promised someone in business more than you could deliver? That's a trap!

Have you thought about having an affair with someone at the office? That's a trap!

You're like the catfish who wandered into the Coke can thinking he could get out anytime he wanted to. The problem is that the fish was not paying attention to his surroundings. He was not thinking about the big picture. He got trapped!

There is also a trap of covetousness and worldliness that won't allow us to be content with what we have. We always want a little more. We don't realize that our possessions can all go away in an instant. I used to collect expensive guns and always wanted more and more. But then 50 of them were destroyed in a single day in a house fire.

There is also a trap of self-pity, and many people fall into it every day. It's tempting to feel sorry for yourself, and you may have a very good reason for feeling bad about your situation! But Jesus says we ought to die to ourselves and live for Him instead.

There are serious consequences and suffering involved whenever we fall into a trap of our own making. Remember, my story was an *accident!* But I've known people who deliberately trapped themselves by what they said and did—and they had no one else to blame for the pain that followed for themselves and their whole family.

Are you caught in a trap right now? My advice is to take God's way out of the trap. It's simple. Cry out to God and let Him walk you through it. That's the very best thing you can do, even if it costs you something to do it.

> *For without cause have they hid for me their net in a pit, which without cause they have digged for my soul. Let destruction come upon him at unawares; and let his net that he hath hid catch himself: into that very destruction let him fall.*
> **Psalm 35:7-8**

> *Whoso causeth the righteous to go astray in an evil way, he shall fall himself into his own pit: but the upright shall have good things in possession.*
> **Proverbs 28:10**

> *Whoso diggeth a pit shall fall therein: and he that rolleth a stone, it will return upon him.*
> **Proverbs 26:27**

Thou art snared with the words of thy mouth, thou art taken with the words of thy mouth. Do this now, my son, and deliver thyself, when thou art come into the hand of thy friend; go, humble thyself, and make sure thy friend.

Proverbs 6:2-3

Parable of Relocating Raccoons

Camille Woods grew a vegetable and herb garden at her home in Dallas, Texas, which was set among many large, mature oak trees in her neighborhood. A creek ran behind her yard. Gardens, trash cans, a creek, and hollow oak trees are the perfect combination to attract raccoons!

Mrs. Woods called me one day to catch some raccoons that had overrun her yard. But she gave me specific instructions to catch and release them and not hurt the animals. So I caught them with big cage traps that featured a door at either end and a bait pan in the center. When a curious raccoon looked into the trap, he saw a way out, which set his mind at ease. However, both doors would close once the raccoon went inside to eat the food.

I captured at least twenty-five raccoons from Mrs. Woods' backyard this way. They were not too happy about being caught. When I relocated the whole bunch to the wild river bottoms of East Texas, they probably weren't happy about that either...at first. But the raccoons would be safer, have better access to food, and enjoy a better habitat than they had in the middle of Dallas! Mrs. Woods was happy and, eventually, so were the relocated raccoons.

Horse-Sense Interpretation

Sometimes God wants to move us to a different level in our spiritual walk with him. That usually means something in our lives has to change. We may have to quit a job we like. We may need to end a friendship. We may even have to move somewhere else!

God will do whatever it takes to move us closer to him. Sometimes if we're stubborn and causing problems, like the raccoons were doing in Dallas, He even allows us to be "caught" so that He can move us to a different location.

However, we don't like change. I like settling into routines myself. When I was a young man in rodeo, I was content— but God moved me out of it. I was also content in a job with the timber industry until God moved me along to the next thing. I also had a very lucrative contract catching alligators for the State of Texas, but God moved me out of it also. We pray for direction in our lives, but when God moves us, we sometimes throw a fit because we don't see that what He is doing is really for our good.

Like the raccoons in this story, we may not be happy about the change at first. But then we realize He is taking us to a place that's actually better for us than where we were before. God knows what He is doing when He shifts you around. His plans for us are good.

> *Trust in the Lord with all thine heart; and lean not unto thine own understanding. In all thy ways acknowledge him, and he shall direct thy paths.*
> **Proverbs 3:5-6**

> *"At that time will I bring you again, even in the time that I gather you: for I will make you a name and a praise among all people of the earth, when I turn back your captivity before your eyes," saith the Lord.*
> **Zephaniah 3:20**

PARABLE OF BEING HUNGRY FOR A BIRD

If it were possible to overdose on pinto beans, I would have definitely been a statistic when I ran out of meat and vegetables one November in the Alaskan wilderness. All I had to eat for three weeks were pinto beans and little pine-tar-tasting red squirrels. Eating pinto beans by themselves with no other food can cause horrible gas explosions and even hallucinations. Or, in my case, at least daydreams of Dr. Pepper, candy bars, and roasted birds.

Since there was nowhere to get Dr. Pepper or candy bars, I eventually had to figure out how to trap some birds to eat. There are at least three types of ptarmigan and grouse in Alaska. The blue grouse tastes like quail and is a wild, dark meat. The rock grouse tastes like chicken and has white meat. The rough grouse tastes like a mixture of chicken and quail. But how would I catch them? After experiencing yet another massive gas attack one day, I opened the door long enough to let some fresh air in and some mice out. That's when I got a bright idea.

The previous summer, I caught salmon in a gill net, and that got me thinking. I washed the gill net until it was white as snow. Then I took some dry pinto beans for bait and headed up the mountain to where the rock ptarmigan had been feeding in some low buttonbush and diamond willow.

Next, I cut some posts and hung the net over an open area of snow on a small mountainside field near the brush. I scattered pinto beans around and hoped for the best.

I left for a few hours and when I returned, two rock ptarmigans were entangled in my net. They got caught in the net when a larger flock flew in to eat the beans, never seeing the white net against the snow.

The next few weeks, I ate ptarmigan and beans. When I was finally able to hike out and sell some of my furs, I stocked up on candy, canned fish, canned and dried fruit, vegetable and *no pinto beans*! A bush pilot airdropped the supplies to me because I couldn't pack all of them in my backpack!

Horse-Sense Interpretation

Just because something looks pure as snow doesn't mean that it is. Ask those birds. The net was invisible against the snow. They should have thought twice about seeing something new and out-of-place like pinto beans in the wilderness. It was a nice snack, but their hunger led to some of them being caught in my trap. Satan, remember, disguises

himself as an angel of light, according to the Bible. If
something is too good to be true or seems too easy, it probably
is. Those beans looked good, but it was a trap!

You know people who fall for payday loans that come
with sky-high interest rates. You also know people who fall
into the trap of paying out a big depreciating purchase like a
mobile home on a 30-year note, instead of managing their
money more wisely. It sounds like a low payment and a steal-
of-a-deal, but it's a trap.

There are traps out there in the world trying to trip you
up by offering something that sounds easy and enjoyable. I
tried the "easy way" many times myself in life, and it did not
work. Use wisdom. Ask God for discernment instead.

*The proud have hid a snare for me, and cords; they
have spread a net by the wayside; they have set gins for
me. Selah.*
Psalm 140:5

*Let the wicked fall into their own nets, whilst that I
withal escape.*
Psalm 141:10

Surely in vain the net is spread in the sight of any bird.
Proverbs 1:17

For such are false apostles, deceitful workers,
transforming themselves into the apostles of Christ.
And no marvel; for Satan himself is transformed into
an angel of light.
2 Corinthians 11:13-14

Lest Satan should get an advantage of us: for we are
not ignorant of his devices.
2 Corinthians 2:11

And forgive us our debts, as we forgive our debtors. And
lead us not into temptation, but deliver us from evil:
For thine is the kingdom, and the power, and the glory,
for ever. Amen.
Matthew 6:12-13

PARABLE OF THE BOBCAT AND THE RACCOON

I sat on a high bank of a river one evening right before dark and observed raccoons traveling by. As I watched, one raccoon saw a beer bottle cap and went to pick it up. Another raccoon grabbed a shiny piece of tin foil that some careless camper had left behind and began playing with it. Those raccoons eventually left, and another group of raccoons came by and did the same thing with the shiny objects. Who knows why? Those objects obviously attracted the raccoon's attention and it gave me an idea. What if I could catch raccoons with aluminum foil? And that got me thinking about another idea.

At the time, the Christmas tree at my cabin was decorated with ornaments. I'd often seen my housecat play with the ones that were hung eye-level to a cat. She boxed at them with her paws, clawed at them and stalked the shiny red and green balls, slinking around them in circles. These colorful decorations fascinated her. As any trapper would ask himself, I thought, "Would these ornaments help me catch a bobcat?"

That winter I took a dozen "number two" foot traps and wrapped aluminum foil on the pan. I set these traps in shallow water in some creeks, sloughs, and ponds. To my surprise, I caught more raccoons on the foil than I did on my bait sets and trail sets combined!

Curiosity killed the 'coons, but would it work on the bobcats? The bobcat often hunts rabbits and field mice on the edge of the forest where a field adjoins it. Often they are difficult to trap in these locations because crows, buzzards, skunks, opossums, and other critters get caught going after the bait before the bobcat comes by.

To test my idea, I decided not to use any bait and instead used Christmas ornaments, hanging them eye-level to a cat, set just off the trail. Before Christmas, I caught ten bobcats. They brought me an average of $125 each in late 1974-75. I was in college and happy that curiosity killed the cat.

Horse-Sense Interpretation

People are naturally curious. They play with reading horoscopes, Ouija boards, fortunetellers, and explore various dark spiritual avenues simply out of curiosity. It seems harmless enough, but it can end in captivity or even death. The Bible clearly teaches us to avoid many of those things.

Teenagers are especially drawn to witchcraft and other evil activities because they think it's fun to scare themselves with something "spooky." But most teenagers haven't had enough life experience to know the reality of death or pain. They trust everything, and they shouldn't.

Curiosity is God-given in order to learn about the world we live in. We learn best with guided leadership from someone older and wiser.

A coyote pup, for example, will follow anything out of curiosity if its left alone in the den. They'll follow a cow or a dog on a farm. And they'll even innocently try to play with a bobcat that is there to eat it for lunch! An eagle can attack a pup outside the den, and the others will stumble out of the safety of their den just to find out what happened. They're curious. And it's deadly. Coyote parents have to teach their young what will harm them if they're not careful.

In the same way, people are out to deceive us in this world. God and the Holy Spirit can lead us in the right way to protect us from harming ourselves and innocently dabbling in evil activities. The Bible says Jesus leads us like a shepherd leads sheep, because sheep will also follow anything or anyone. Unmanaged curiosity is dangerous. Follow Christ and you'll stay out of trouble.

Therefore hearken not ye to your prophets, nor to your diviners, nor to your dreamers, nor to your enchanters, nor to your sorcerers, which speak unto you, saying, Ye shall not serve the king of Babylon.
Jeremiah 27:9

There shall not be found among you any one that maketh his son or his daughter to pass through the fire, or that useth divination, or an observer of times, or an enchanter, or a witch. Or a charmer, or a consulter with familiar spirits, or a wizard, or a necromancer. For all that do these things are an abomination unto the Lord: and because of these abominations the Lord thy God doth drive them out from before thee.
Deuteronomy 18:10-12

And hath gone and served other gods, and worshipped them, either the sun, or moon, or any of the host of heaven, which I have not commanded.
Deuteronomy 17:3

Thou art wearied in the multitude of thy counsels. Let now the astrologers, the stargazers, the monthly prognosticators, stand up, and save thee from these things that shall come upon thee.
Isaiah 47:13-14

PARABLE OF THE SMART FOX

Foxes are interesting creatures. They like to bury their excess food, and they also try to steal other foxes' buried food. A fox will dig a little hole in the dirt about 12 inches deep at a 45-degree angle and lightly cover the sparrow or rabbit they did not finish eating to save it for later.

To trap a fox, I would dig a similar hole and place a bird or a piece of rabbit meat in it. Then I would place a foot trap directly in front of the hole and camouflage it. I would catch most fox this way. Then one day I met a real smart fox.

I could not entice this fox with food or even the sexual scent of a female fox in heat. Nor could I catch him using hidden trail sets where he was supposed to innocently walk over the trap. In fact, I couldn't use any other sets I normally used to catch this fox.

This fox was so intelligent that he found all my carefully camouflaged steel traps—without stepping on a single one of them. He would simply dig up a trap, gently turn it upside down (often without tripping it), and take the bait. To my frustration, he would sit down and eat the snack right beside the trap. I put multiple traps at my sets to try to catch him, but he just mocked me every day, stealing my bait and uncovering my traps. That smart fox got away with this bold behavior for about a month.

One winter's night, I thought of a great set to outsmart this fox. I took an old pocket watch and buried it about a foot deep in a plowed, sandy field. Next, I placed a trap set upside down with a light trigger about ten inches under the sand. Then I waited.

A fox can hear 100 times better than a human. It can hear mice digging through leaves or a rat eating corn up to half a mile away. Three days went by with this smart fox circling the field and tripping my other sets like normal. However, each day he also heard that mysterious ticking sound underground and it drove him crazy. Finally, when he couldn't stand it anymore, his curiosity made him dig up the watch.

As was his careful custom, he sensed the trap. And like he had successfully done so many times before, he dug under it to safely reach his paw around and flip the trap over. But since my trap was already upside down, the smart fox was finally outsmarted! Soon his fur was on my stretcher, and he was history in the land.

Horse-Sense Interpretation

After a man has practiced disobedience and rebellion for many years, he thinks he is very clever. He thinks he's gotten away with breaking God's laws and believes he will never be caught.

Our nation and our government are full of smart foxes. Over time, they learn to work the system in their favor. They steal, lie, and mock judgement—seemingly without consequence. And nothing bad ever happens to them! So they become more and more arrogant, showing off their skillful wickedness. They don't realize that God is being merciful, waiting for them to repent of their evil ways.

However, we cannot outsmart God. He has a pocket watch somewhere. And it's ticking. Consider this a warning and change your ways. Everyone is eventually caught and brought to judgement—in this life or in the next.

> *He hath said in his heart, "God hath forgotten: He hideth his face, he will never see it." Wherefore doth the wicked contemn (revile) God? He hath said in his heart, "Thou wilt not require it."*
> **Psalm 10:11, 13**

For I was envious at the foolish when I saw the prosperity of the wicked. Until I went into the sanctuary of God, then understood I their end. Surely thou didst set them in slippery places; thou castedst them down in destruction. How are they brought desolation, as in a moment! they are utterly consumed with terror.
Psalm 73:3, 17-19

...For God resisteth the proud and giveth grace to the humble. Humble yourself therefore under the mighty hand of God, that he may exalt you in due time. Casting all your care upon him; for he careth for you. Be sober, be vigilant; because your adversary the devil, as a roaring lion, walketh about, seeking whom he may devour.
1 Peter 5:5-8

PARABLE OF THE WOLF AND FALSE HOPE

Trapping wolves is tricky. I used to tie my traps to a strong tree that would not move, whenever I needed to trap a wolf. But a trapped wolf wants his freedom so much that he will often chew off his own foot, even if he must run away on only three feet. The same trap would not badly damage a tame dog that accidentally stepped in my trap. He would not fight the trap. The dog would just howl and wait patiently for his owner to come and set him free. Sometimes the dog would even fall asleep next to the trap, not moving an inch until his owner arrived. He knew his owner loved him and would be looking for him soon.

I finally figured out that if I put my trap on a smaller weight that the wolf could drag, he would not chew off his foot. Instead, he would drag the weight with him and just *think* he was free. But the wolf never got away because the weight never allowed him enough freedom to go far—just enough to think he was getting away from the trap. The weight deceived him—and that deceit cost the wolf his life. Having this false hope put his fur on my drying frame.

But the problem with the weighted trap was that if I accidentally caught a dog, he did the same foolish thing the wolf did. He would not howl for his owner to help him because the dog also wrongly believed he could free himself. Instead of seeking help from someone who could truly free him, he made it worse for himself.

Horse-Sense Interpretation

Man thinks he can handle his own problem and that he doesn't need God. He often figures that he got himself into this mess, so he can get himself out of it! You may see people dragging around their addictions, sins, problems, and needs all the time—thinking they are able to free themselves anytime they want to. Only they're never truly able to get free from those burdens. Sometimes they even get used to the weight of their problems. Dragging them around is a form of self-punishment for all the things they have done wrong in life. Sometimes they say they "don't want to bother God" with their sin and addictions.

The Bible says Jesus has redeemed us from our sin—He has taken on the punishment for sin so we don't have to! False hope and pride prevents a man for asking for help from a

God who could truly set him free. He would rather remain in pain than ask for help.

Instead of thinking you can get yourself out of the trap you're in, God offers to set you free right now. Cry out to Him, like a beloved dog who is in trouble will cry out to his master. Confess your sin and come to Him for forgiveness. The weight you are carrying is too much for you—and you can never be free from it on your own. God wants to carry your burdens for you because He loves you.

> *Come unto me, all ye that labor and are heavy laden, and I will give you rest.*
> **Matthew 11:28**

> *If the son therefore shall make you free, ye shall be free indeed.*
> **John 8:36**

> *The way of the fool if right in his own eyes; but he that hearkeneth unto counsel is wise.*
> **Proverbs 12:15**

> *Seek ye the Lord while he may be found, call ye upon him while he is near. Let the wicked forsake his way, and the unrighteous man his thoughts; and let him return to the Lord and he will have mercy upon him; and to our God for he will abundantly pardon.*
> **Isaiah 55:6-7**

For my thoughts are not your thoughts, neither are your ways my ways, saith the Lord. For as the heavens are higher than the earth, so are my ways higher than your ways, and my thoughts than your thoughts.

Isaiah 55:8-9

PARABLE OF MICE
IN MY CABIN

When I was living in Alaska, I planned my trip very well, but I neglected to buy mousetraps. It was a two-day hike to the nearest village to buy more supplies, and it was extremely cold. Not wanting to break a new trail in six feet of snow, hiking north against the bitter wind, I figured it would be okay. But I was not prepared for the explosion of mice in my cabin!

The only thing I had with me were large animal traps and absolutely no mousetraps. The population dynamics of these mice are such that they were breeding every 28 days with 8-10 young. The young reproduced every 90 days. That's a lot of mice. My log cabin was soon overrun with these little guys.

As I saw it, I had three possible solutions to the mouse problem. One, I could trap a live mink and release it in my cabin. Two, I could shoot the mice with my .22 revolver. Three, I could design my own trap for mice.

Initially, I went with option one and caught a nice mink in a homemade box trap. I released the mink into the cabin, and it proved to be a good mouser—for about one week. When it had had enough, the mink pulled the moss away from between two logs of my outer wall and escaped. I moved on to option two.

I read my Bible in the evenings and practiced my Billy the Kid quick draw with my .22 pistol. After going through four boxes of shells, and suffering a badly damaged wall in my cabin, I had only killed one mouse in two months. All the excitement only made the mice breed more! I was a trapper in deep trouble because I did not pack a simple mousetrap in my supplies.

Moving to my last option, I designed my first mousetrap out of a bucket, but I only caught one mouse a week. The population of mice peaked, and I reached my wit's end. But one day by accident I invented another mousetrap that saved my cabin and my sanity!

Several times a week I cooked pancakes and syrup. After my meal, I washed my only plate, fork, and spoon and put the leftovers outside for my dogs. One morning I forgot to clean my plate and left it in the sink to go hunting moose (not mice) for the day. When I returned home that evening, I made an amazing discovery. Eleven mice were stuck in the gooey syrup left on my plate from the morning! Some mice were smothered to death in the ecstasy of the sweet maple syrup, and others were still alive but stuck fast to the plate.

The rest of the winter, I used that plate and maple syrup to catch mice, and I ate my meals out of my gold-sifting pan. I wish I would have patented my mouse trap because later it became the popular glue trap!

Horse-Sense Interpretation

In life, we all get caught in sticky situations from time to time. We need a friend like Jesus who can pull us out. Are you caught in sticky circumstances you can't escape? Let Jesus unstick you!

Like the mice in this story, sometimes our biggest problems start out with something sweet and appealing. For example, maybe you're offered more money at work if you'll just compromise your integrity a tiny bit and change some numbers on a report. The money sounds great, so maybe you dive in headfirst. And then you find out you're stuck in a situation you can't get out of.

You can't get away from trouble on your own. You can struggle and strain, but it's not going to happen. The temptation is to compromise your way out of a sticky situation and rationalize your behavior. You'll think to yourself that it's going okay—it's not that big of a deal. But before you know it, you're hopelessly stuck in sin.

I once knew a man who went to jail for selling drugs. He became a devoted follower of Christ in jail, but he was afraid of what might happen to him when he returned to society. This man owed some very bad people money, and they were waiting for him when he got out. He sought me for advice, and I suggested to him that he had three options in this sticky situation. One, he could run away, but they would find him. Two, he could try to negotiate with them, but that was unlikely to work. Three, he could go on the offensive and tell them straight up that he would pay them back because he was a Christian now. He chose that third option and boldly told the bad guys that if they went after him, God would go after them! Long story short, he paid his dues and today he's still following Christ. God had to unstick him from his circumstances.

> *I sink in deep mire, where there is no standing: I am come into deep waters, where the floods overflow me.*
> **Psalm 69:2**

> *Deliver me out of the mire, and let me not sink: let me be delivered from them that hate me, and out of the deep waters.*
> **Psalm 69:14**

> *He brought me up also out of an horrible pit, out of the miry clay, and set my feet upon a rock, and established my goings. And he hath put a new song in my mouth, even praise unto our God: many shall see it, and fear, and shall trust in the Lord.*
>
> **Psalm 40:2-3**

PARABLE OF THE NERVOUS AND CONFUSED QUAIL

An old gentleman named Henry Dowel lived in Golden, Texas. He and my father 'coon hunted together, along with my brothers and me. He owned some bottomland in the Sabine River bottom, as well as the farmland uphill from the river. Henry taught me a little about trapping and netting fish, but he also taught me about the goodness of God.

One day he was making a wire pen that looked like a lady's hat box. It was eight inches high and thirty-six inches around, with no apparent door except a 6x6 square hole cut in the bottom center of the pen.

I watched him working and asked, "Sir, what is that going to be?"

"A quail trap," he answered. I had never seen a trap quite like that one, and I was curious how it worked.

When Henry laid the bottom of the pen flat against the ground, I said, "A quail can't get in that!"

He just smiled and started digging a shallow ditch about three feet long. Then he poured what looked like millet or maize in the ditch and positioned the hole in the trap over the end of the ditch.

"Looky here," he told me. "The quail will come out of that plum thicket over there, jump in this little trough, follow that grain, and jump right up into the trap. All it will take is one quail to go first, and all the others will follow him."

"It won't work, Henry," I said, shaking my head. "All those quail have to do to escape is go back to the center of your trap, jump down through the hole, and walk out. Easy as pie, the quail will be free! It won't work—no way!"

Henry laughed. "They could do exactly what you say, Mark. But they won't, because they will be nervous and confused. You watch—they'll be running around in circles inside that pen, looking everywhere but down. Occasionally, one will even run across the center of the pen, hopping right over the hole, just to run around and around the edge again!"

I wasn't convinced, but to my surprise Henry did catch a whole covey of quail in a day or so!

He later explained that once in a while he would run across an unusual quail that wasn't nervous or confused. That calm quail would quietly make this way to the center of the pen and find the way out through the hole in the bottom. He was free, but he wouldn't run away. That quail would cry and chirp into the hole for the others to join him until, one by one, they were all free.

Horse-Sense Interpretation

When you are afraid, nervous, and confused, you won't be able to escape a problem or crisis you find yourself in. You'll just run around in circles all day, having panic attacks and scrambling for solutions that don't work! Instead, go to the center of the trap, be still, and let the love of Jesus clear your mind.

Jesus is full of love, mercy, wisdom, and knowledge—and he's waiting *in the center* of your problem. He is not afraid, nervous, or confused. Go to him, and abide with Jesus in the middle of your trap (a.k.a. your situation). Do not try to get out. Just abide in his peace and his love, and he will guide you.

The next time you are feeling afraid and confused in a crisis, calm down and wait on Jesus in the middle of your problem. This advice is something I've learned by experience—and it's rooted in the love of God.

People fear condemnation, so they often bypass Jesus' offer of help. They keep running around in circles, jumping right over the way of escape—just like those quail. Other people mistakenly think they have to work to get themselves out of the mess they're in *before* Jesus will help them. But Jesus can be with you *while* your life is messed up. He *wants* to be with you in the middle of the problem. That's why the Bible says that Jesus took on our sin on the cross—because He loves us. He's the only one who can help us.

> *For God is not the author of confusion, but of peace, as in all churches of the saints.*
> **1 Corinthians 14:33**

> *For God hath not given us the spirit of fear; but of power, and of love, and of a sound mind.*
> **2 Timothy 1:7**

> *Peace I leave with you, my peace I give unto you: not as the world giveth, give I unto you. Let not your heart be troubled, neither let it be afraid.*
> **John 14:27**

> *That he would grant you, according to the riches of his glory, to be strengthened with might by his Spirit in the inner man; That Christ may dwell in your hearts by faith; that ye, being rooted and grounded in love, May be able to comprehend with all saints what is the*

breadth, and length, and depth, and height; And to know the love of Christ, which passeth knowledge, that ye might be filled with all the fulness of God. Now unto him that is able to do exceeding abundantly above all that we ask or think, according to the power that worketh in us, Unto him be glory in the church by Christ Jesus throughout all ages, world without end. Amen.

Ephesians 3:16-21

And the Lord direct your hearts into the love of God, and into the patient waiting for Christ.

2 Thessalonians 3:5

PARABLE OF THE GREAT COYOTE TRAPPER

I thought I was a great coyote trapper because I once snared 118 coyotes in six months on a ranch in Texas. Then I heard a rumor about a man in New Mexico named Wes who put my skills to shame.

According to the stories my friends told me, I was merely an amateur compared to this trapper named Wes. Wes trapped in the Desert Mountains near the Mascalero Apache Indian Reservation in New Mexico. Because of his reputation and his experience with Indians, he was offered the opportunity to make authentic Indian clothes, artifacts, and fur clothing for Robert Redford's movie *Jeremiah Johnson* about a Mexican-American war veteran who sets out to spend time alone in the wilderness. In the movie, a wiser and more experienced outdoorsman takes Redford under his wing to show him how to survive. I felt much like Redford when I drove to New Mexico in hopes of meeting Wes. A friend and good trapper named Ricky Roger introduced me to this legendary trapper. Wes and his wife had a half-dozen of what looked like family albums spread on the coffee table in their home. The albums contained incredible pictures of Wes with an entire family of coyotes caught in a single area, a family of bobcats in another set, and another whole family of coyotes in another set.

Wes hadn't caught the coyotes one at a time, like I was doing. He caught *every* coyote in the mountain range in each set location! I saw pictures of 300-square-foot areas with nine coyotes caught. There were at least twenty photographs of four to seven coyotes caught in each bunch set. This is highly unusual and very difficult to do. I realized Wes was a great coyote trapper and I needed to be quiet and learn his tricks.

I do not remember everything Wes said, but I recall most of it. "Mark," he told me, "you know coyotes travel together, hunt together, play together, and sleep together. So why do you try to trap just one at a set?"

I did not have an answer for him.

Wes explained that there are places in the desert mountains where several trails crossed. He had observed how the coyotes went to these intersections to socialize, sing, look for a mate, eat, and get in fights with other males to prove who is dominant.

In these high-traffic areas, they are less aware of their surroundings. They're often showing off for each other and not paying attention. Here in these special areas, the coyote loses his keen wisdom and general wariness. Wes used this behavior against the coyotes to trap them all at once.

What I learned from Wes that day was to scatter small bits of bait with absolutely no traps near the bait. I make it extra tantalizing by chopping up rattlesnake and bobcat meat and frying it in bacon grease. I keep my bait 200 yards or so from the trail intersections, but I throw it generously on all the trails going to the intersection.

The bait is small enough and scattered widely enough for each family member and friend of the coyotes to stop and hunt for the bait. After a while, they continue to the socializing intersection where the party is!

I have placed several traps in one small area of this intersection. I do not need to put food or bait in this area. Instead, I use the urine of a female coyote in heat and spray it liberally on every cactus, bush, or fencepost. Each bush in this small area has a separate scent from a different female coyote that wants to breed. I am careful not to leave any human scent. I sit on a horse blanket to do my work and use a sand sifter to cover my sets, making it look totally natural. The male coyotes can smell this irresistible scent from a distance, causing them to howl and attract females as they challenge other males to a fight.

After all the coyotes bark and howl for their buddies to join them, they travel together down to the intersection to socialize and breed.

Soon, a single coyote is caught.

If he were caught on the trail, the trail would be avoided by all. But since I catch him in an area where there is so much fun going on, the other coyotes ignore what happened to their friend. They keep carrying on with their prideful ways, seducing the females and partying. They are distracted trying to find the females who left that scent. Sometimes the coyotes even compete and fight over a set before they're caught.

A coyote that's caught can usually count on his true friends and family to come help him out. And guess what? They get trapped, too. Some of the female coyotes are so desperate to breed that they come to the trapped males. The male will even howl and try to call her closer to him— forgetting all about the fact that he's trapped. That's how I catch the females, too.

After I met Wes and learned how to catch coyotes this way, I felt like a fool for trapping them one at a time on trails or feeding areas. Now that I've learned a new way, I can catch 90% of the coyotes in an area.

There are always a few loners who are exceptions to the rule. They do not follow their natural instincts, and I am not able to trap them no matter what I try. I like to think they learned something from watching their pals suffer so much destruction.

Horse-Sense Interpretation

The scene I described about the coyotes is the same scene that plays out any Friday night in America. A guy and his buddies go get a pizza and hang out at someone's home. The girls come over for a visit, and eventually everyone heads downtown to a dance club or bar. They're on the cell phones on the way there, calling everyone they know to join them. At the club, everyone's guard is down and they're all caught up in the moment.

It seems like fun for a while, but many end up trapped in unwanted pregnancy, abortion, sexually transmitted disease, fights, bad relationships, addictions—and some end up dying. Nobody means for that to happen. All of them want to just have some fun and look for love (or lust).

Some people are blind to danger. And some people, like the wise loner coyote I've observed, watch from a distance and choose to avoid danger at all costs. They refuse to go to those types of places. Instead of being lured into sin with all their friends, they turn from danger and run!

My son, if sinners entice thee, consent thou not.
Proverbs 1:10

To deliver thee from the strange woman, even from the stranger that flattereth with her words.
Proverbs 2:16

None that go unto her return again, neither take they hold of the paths of life. That thou mayest walk in the way of good men, and keep the paths of the righteous.
Proverbs 2:19-20

Enter not into the path of the wicked, and go not in the way of evil men. Avoid it, pass not by it, turn from it and pass away.
Proverbs 4:14-15

For the lips of a strange woman drop as an honeycomb, and her mouth is smoother than oil. Her feet go down to death; her steps take hold on hell. Remove thy way far from her, and come not nigh the door of her house:
Proverbs 5:3, 5, 8

Lust not after her beauty in thine heart; neither let her take thee with her eyelids. Can a man take fire in his bosom, and his clothes not be burned?
Proverbs 6:25, 27

I have perfumed my bed with myrrh, aloes, and cinnamon. Let not thine heart decline to her ways, go not astray in her paths. For she hath cast down many wounded: yea, many strong men have been slain by her.

Proverbs 7:17, 25-26

Trust in the Lord with all thine heart; and lean not unto thine own understanding. In all thy ways acknowledge him, and he shall direct thy paths. Be not wise in thine own eyes: fear the Lord, and depart from evil.

Proverbs 3:5-7

My son, let not them depart from thine eyes: keep sound wisdom and discretion. Then shalt thou walk in thy way safely, and thy foot shall not stumble. For the Lord shall be thy confidence, and shall keep thy foot from being taken.

Proverbs 3:21, 23, 26

But I say unto you, that whosoever looketh on a woman to lust after her hath committed adultery with her already in his heart.

Matthew 5:28, The Lord Jesus

Watch ye and pray, lest ye enter into temptation. The spirit truly is ready, but the flesh is weak.

Mark 14:38, The Lord Jesus

PARABLE OF
THE EVIL STUD HORSE

U sually I trap fur-bearing animals, but occasionally someone hires me to catch livestock and move them elsewhere. I rode saddle broncs and bulls for many years, and I love rodeos and riding a good cow horse. It's no surprise that I have always owned a few riding horses, even when I lived in the city. Several of my friends kept horses on a 100-acre pasture in Dallas, including my gelding, mare, and a colt. One day the landowner called me in a panic. Some crazy black stallion had killed two geldings and three colts. It had even stolen about fifteen mares who followed him off our pasture to an unknown location. Afraid I'd lost my animals, I asked if my horses were among the casualties, but the landowner did not know.

I contacted a cowboy friend of mine named Steve to come with me to find the stolen mares. If possible, I wanted to try to save the other horses from this evil black stud horse. When we arrived on the property, I was happy to find my gelding was safe and alive with another mare. We quickly saddled the horses to head out looking for the stolen remuda. But we would soon become the hunted, no longer the hunters.

We eventually saw the black stallion from afar, and when he saw us he came running at us full-throttle and all teeth! Poor Steve tried to rope the evil creature, but it rammed right into Steve's horse. Before I could do anything, the stallion bit Steve on the shoulder, lifted him off his horse, and shook him like a bulldog shaking a dead cat. After what seemed like an eternity, the stallion dropped Steve on the ground and reared up on its hind legs, preparing to stomp my friend to death. At my command, my horse charged. Thanks to God and my obedient horse, we helped Steve get away just in time.

The two horses fought neck-to-neck in a fury, but my horse was at a disadvantage. For one thing, it could not bite the stallion because of the bit in its mouth. The stud was also twice as strong and fast as my horse. But one very important thing in my horse's favor was that the cowboy in the saddle had a whip and could ride!

The wild stud pawed viciously at me and tried to strike a deadly blow, but I rode sideways while whipping him in the face. Whenever that evil horse bit my horse, I spurred his face and whipped at his neck. We fought like this for what seemed like hours. It was like fighting two dinosaurs and a grizzly bear at the same time! All three of us—the stallion, my horse, and me—were soaked in blood and sweat. When I had the opportunity to make a small charge at the stallion, I caught him sideways and knocked him down.

When he got up again, he was furious! Steve had made it back to the truck by this time and was attempting to drive out of the pasture to get help (or a gun). He left the horse trailer behind and gassed the truck. While Steve was driving away, that sorry stud horse pawed at the truck's hood and kicked out the windshield before "Wham!"—my obedient horse suddenly knocked the stud down again. I was flying high on an adrenaline rush at this point. I took my whip and my horse and I drove this wild black stallion into the empty horse trailer. Looking back, I think he was actually relieved to get away from my old obedient horse and hide from my whip.

I leaped off my horse and locked the trailer. We were all completely exhausted. I was so proud of my old horse who had done the impossible, even though it was not half as strong and not nearly as mean as that devil creature now inside the trailer. My horse defeated and captured the stallion for one reason—and only one reason: my horse obeyed my every command. I had the skill and technique to fight the stallion, not to mention a whip. Instinctively, my horse knew that the more dangerous a situation was, the more obedient it had to be to survive. My old horse trusted me more than its own ability or experience—and together, we won against the enemy.

You could not pay me one million dollars to go through that horse fight again! At the same time, you couldn't pay me two million *not* to have experienced it!

Horse-Sense Interpretation

Satan came to kill, steal, and destroy. He is a powerful angel, the Bible says—much more powerful, smart, evil, and cruel than any of us. That's a picture of the evil stud horse who kidnapped our horses and killed many others before we stopped him.

If we try to fight Satan in a spiritual battle using our own strength, we will be destroyed—or at least enslaved by him to do his bidding. Like my aging horse, we are simply not strong enough to do battle with the devil on our own.

We must instead let God control our tongue, obey His commands, and respond to His guidance. He is the skilled cowboy, moving in our lives and guiding us like God clearly says in His Word He will do. God will take us in our weakness and use His infinite skill to drive the enemy away and keep us safe from harm.

It's pretty simple. We trust and obey—and we are victorious!

If you love me, keep my commandments.
John 14:15

Ye are my friends, if you do whatsoever I command you.
John 15:14

But if thou shall indeed obey his voice, and do all that I speak; I will be an enemy unto thine enemies, and an adversary unto thine adversaries.
Exodus 23:2

So he fed them according to the integrity of his heart; and guided them by the skillfulness of his hands.
Psalm 78:72

Casting down imaginations, and every high thing that exalteth itself against the knowledge of God; and bringing into captivity every thought to the obedience of Christ; And having in readiness to revenge all disobedience, when your obedience is fulfilled.
2 Corinthians 10:5-6

Be strong and of good courage, fear not, nor be afraid of them; for thy Lord thy God, He it is that doth go with thee; He will not fail thee, nor forsake thee.
Deuteronomy 31:6

PARABLE OF
THE JEALOUS, BUSY BEAVERS

One day I received a phone call from an oil company with a problem. They could not get down the service roads to check their oil wells because beavers had plugged three culverts and built a dam, flooding the alternative roads.

This was a case of nuisance wildlife control that required all the beavers to be removed. A government-hired trapper was called in and he caught two beavers—one that was one year old and one that was two. But he was unable to finish the job because of his busy schedule. The oil company then hired me to take over. Judging from the age of the hut and the beavers that had been removed, I knew there were still six to eight beavers left to trap.

Beavers mate for life and are very territorial. Only the husband, wife, and children live in each family's well-defined territory. They will fight off, drive away, or even kill any intruder. The maximum size of a family (called a colony) is ten beavers. That family requires about twenty acres of habitat. The adult Momma and Papa beaver have a scent gland under their tail that excretes oil and castor. Papa and Momma travel to all the corners of their property, pile up mud and leaves on the shoreline, and excrete scent to warn other beavers not to trespass.

Beavers cannot breed until they are three-and-a-half or four years old. They will have two to four babies a year and keep the youngsters in the family for the first two-and-a-half years. Then the parents will run off those children to force them to find mates and begin a family elsewhere.

The work I needed to do would be more difficult than a typical beaver job. If I didn't get the parents right at the start, it might be a very long, drawn out job to get them all. Once the parents sense danger, they educate the young and keep them from harm. In this particular situation, the wary parents were on to me already, having lost two kids to the government worker's traps! It was essential to first trap Momma and Papa, leaving all the others unguided, unprotected, and vulnerable to my traps.

Knowing beavers are jealous hard workers with quick tempers, I came up with a plan after I analyzed the problem area. Keeping these weaknesses in mind, I was certain I could trap the parents and the entire family in no time.

I made no sets on the trails, den entrances, or feed areas. I didn't want to catch the younger beavers yet—just their parents. So I decided to do the old soap opera trick. I call it my Peyton Place set, named after the popular 1960s serial of the same name. I took castor from a female beaver on a job site many miles away and sprinkled it right on Papa beaver's scent mound. Then I took castor from a male beaver that I'd caught miles away and put it on Momma beaver's scent mound. Then I set two traps and waited for the drama to begin!

The next morning, I had a 50-pound, six-year-old jealous Momma beaver in my trap. She had put herself in danger when she thought Papa had been messing around with another lady beaver! That was one less parent to guard the offspring and one step closer to getting all the beavers in that family. Surprisingly, Papa beaver had been so busy building dams that he hadn't gotten jealous of the unfamiliar male scent on Momma's scent mound. He hadn't even visited my set. He was a workaholic and hadn't noticed that Momma beaver was gone!

So I switched strategies for Papa beaver and used his workaholic nature to my advantage. I tore two big holes in his dam. Then I set two traps near a peeled stick that I stabbed in the mud, knowing he would see the stick and use it to start the dam repair. By the next morning, I had five-year-old Papa beaver and one two-year-old in my traps. The rest of the day, with both parents out of the picture, I set up den entrance sets, trail sets, dam repair sets, and exploring sets. By the third morning, I had the other five younger beavers and was ready to call it a day.

Horse-Sense Interpretation

If Satan can divide Momma and Papa, he can destroy the children. Using human weaknesses like jealousy, unforgiveness, anger, worry, and workaholic tendencies, he can erode marriage bonds and destroy a family in no time.

That is why it is so important to obey Christ's commands and love one another, forgive one another, and be kind to one another. It's essential that parents teach their children about the dangers of jealousy, greed, unforgiveness, selfishness, and hatred.

Parents must also teach them about trusting God. For mothers and fathers, that might mean repenting from being a worry wart in front of the kids. It might mean asking your family to forgive you for neglecting them because you are a workaholic. Commit to spend more time with your family. A bigger house, another car, or earning more prestige for yourself may sound good, but it may be a trap. Not trusting your spouse—or giving your spouse reason not to trust you—

is also a trap. Many a marriage has been destroyed by false accusations.

Both parties in a marriage relationship are often trapped by their own weaknesses and then the whole family suffers. Let's protect and love our children and save marriages one by one.

> *Set me as a seal upon thine heart, as a seal upon thine arm: for love is strong as death; jealousy is cruel as the grave: the coals thereof are coals of fire, which hath a most vehement flame.*
> **Song of Solomon 8:6**

> *For jealousy is the rage of a man: therefore he will not spare in the day of vengeance.*
> **Proverbs 6:34**

> *The simple believeth every word: but the prudent man looketh well to his going. A wise man feareth, and departeth from evil: but the fool rageth, and is confident. He that is soon angry dealeth foolishly: and a man of wicked devices is hated.*
> **Proverbs 14:15-17**

> *The discretion of a man deferreth his anger; and it is his glory to pass over a transgression.*
> **Proverbs 19:11**

O that there were such an heart in them, that they would fear me, and keep all my commandments always, that it might be well with them, and with their children for ever!
Deuteronomy 5:29

Rejoice, and be exceeding glad: for great is your reward in heaven: for so persecuted they the prophets which were before you.
Matthew 5:12

PARABLE OF
THE HANDICAPPED FOX

I met one fox in my life that I never could catch. This fox did not act like a natural fox. It never buried its food, was not real curious, and only ate what he caught that day or some fruit still on the vine or tree.

This fox had none of a natural fox's bad habits. For example, it never stole another fox's food. It also mated with only one female, never seemed to be in a rush, and wasn't defensive about his territory. While a typical red fox roams about 1,000 acres for hunting, this fox never roamed more than 300 yards from where he slept.

I didn't understand why this fox was so different, but I was amazed that he was so content.

The fox and I saw each other every day for four years during trapping season in a small patch of woods in Dallas, Texas, near White Rock Lake. He rested on a flat place of an oak tree branch that had broken about 15 feet up the trunk and arched over my hiking trail. Carefully hidden in the camouflage of the tree leaves, the fox felt safe. I never saw him outside of his camouflage, but I knew he was there because I could often see part of an ear or his tail.

Perched high on that tree branch, this fox seemed to enjoy watching me set traps in his feeding area. The fox knew every set and was not tempted in any way. He ignored them, keeping a safe distance from each one. I tried to catch this amazing fox for two years and finally gave up because he was so clever. I figured he was about seven or eight years old, which is far past the four or five years of a normal fox's lifespan.

One day I noticed the fox was peacefully asleep as I passed under that branch on my daily hike through the woods to go to work trapping other animals. So I decided to quietly climb up the tree and surprise this old fox. To my surprise, I crept right next to him without waking him up and even reached out and touched him as he slept soundly. His nose was burned, most likely from a forest fire. One eye was blind, and he could barely hear because part of his ear was missing. This poor fox could only see in one eye, could not smell, and was nearly deaf in one ear–and it still outsmarted me. I climbed down the tree and let him sleep. My best friend, Mark Couch, watched the entire ordeal—so everything I saw that day is true and I have a witness! It was a rare encounter with nature I'll never forget.

This handicapped fox was wise enough to watch me set my traps, would not steal, was true to his mate, got plenty of rest, did not hoard food, was not greedy, and was content with his daily provisions. The fox lived a simple, content, and humble life. I reckon that one day I'll see him again in Heaven, along with whatever other critters will be there.

Horse-Sense Interpretation

Someone who lives at peace doesn't long for the things of the world. They don't steal, they don't lie, they can be true to their mate, and they trust God for daily provisions. In other words, they live a contented life. Being thankful to get by with what you have is a good way to live. Those who are discontent never have enough, and they're unhappy.

A smart person also recognizes his weakness and limitations (like the fox) and watches the enemy closely to avoid getting hurt. That fox never worried about my traps because he saw where I put them and avoided each one. Since he was filled with wisdom and understanding—and he was content—he slept peacefully. Jesus told us to "watch and pray"—and that's exactly what we need to do every day. Satan is no match for even the weakest Christians with all their flaws when they trust God to protect them.

If we stay humble and meek, the Bible promises that we will receive God's mercy and inherit the blessings of God. Plus, sometimes we'll get blessings we didn't even expect.

Surely in vain the net is spread in the sight of any bird.
Proverbs 1:17

Wherefore he saith, Awake thou that sleepest, and arise from the dead, and Christ shall give thee light. See then that ye walk circumspectly, not as fools, but as wise, redeeming the time, because the days are evil. Wherefore be ye not unwise, but understanding what the will of the Lord is.
Ephesians 5:14-17

For as a snare shall it come on all them that dwell on the face of the whole earth. Watch ye therefore, and pray always, that ye may be accounted worthy to escape all these things that shall come to pass, and to stand before the Son of man.
Luke 21:35-36

Lest Satan should get an advantage of us: for we are not ignorant of his devices.
2 Corinthians 2:11

*But God hath chosen the foolish things of the world to
confound the wise; and God hath chosen the weak
things of the world to confound the things which are
mighty;*
1 Corinthians 1:27

*And he said unto me, My grace is sufficient for thee: for
my strength is made perfect in weakness. Most gladly
therefore will I rather glory in my infirmities, that the
power of Christ may rest upon me.*
2 Corinthians 12:9

*Not that I speak in respect of want: for I have learned,
in whatsoever state I am, therewith to be content.*
Philippians 4:11

Blessed are the meek: for they shall inherit the earth.
Matthew 5:5

*Happy is the man that findeth wisdom, and the man
that getteth understanding. Then shalt thou walk in
thy way safely, and thy foot shall not stumble. When
thou liest down, thou shalt not be afraid: yea, thou
shalt lie down, and thy sleep shall be sweet.*
Proverbs 3:13, 23-24

PARABLE OF
THE STUPID GREEN OPOSSUM

The Texas opossum is the easiest animal to trap. It is a very stupid creature with a great sense of smell, good eyesight, keen hearing—and it eats anything and everything.

If you are trapping opossums, the first thing you want to use for bait is some very rotten eggs. That will call opossums long-distance! It's not even necessary to camouflage the set, make an effort to hide human scent, avoid smoking or chewing tobacco, or take any other precautions to trap opossums. They are that stupid.

Because they're so food-driven, the opossum poses a problem tripping the good sets that I make for trapping fox. Fox sets take a lot of effort—they're sterile, time-consuming, and extremely natural in appearance. It is aggravating to have a forty-dollar fox set tripped by a one-dollar opossum. The only reason I ever skinned an opossum for a dollar was because I didn't want to catch it again! And sometimes it wasn't even worth the dollar to catch them, so I turned them loose.

One evening I was complaining to my good friend Mark Couch that I had not been catching any fox, only many opossums. My friend laughed and declared, "You are just catching the same opossum over and over again!"

I was stunned and a little doubtful. How could I find out for sure?

My friend came up with the idea to dye the next opossum we caught using green hair dye from a local costume shop. Sure enough, we caught one and dyed its fur. "Let's see if we catch him again," Mark suggested and released the green animal to see how many times he would end up in our trap.

We caught him four days in a row with the same trap— the same location and the same bait! We felt sorry for him by then and didn't skin it because who would want green fur?

This took place in the middle of the 1970s when wages were extremely low —only $1.50 to $3.00 per hour. But the fur prices were very high! I could make a month's wages in one week of trapping. The highest-paying fur of all was bobcat at $75. There was a bobcat in the location where I was trapping, but I could not catch him because that stupid green opossum always got there first!

I finally became discouraged and pulled all my traps from that area. A week later, I told Mark I still was not able to catch the bobcat because of the green opossum. He just looked at me and said, "Isn't a possum supposed to be the stupidest animal?"

I nodded.

"Then we ought to be able to outsmart him," he said and went on to explain a creative way to catch the bobcat and take the opossum out of the picture. His plan involved using a large cage trap baited with a live rooster in a separate cage on top of the larger trap. We gave the rooster food and water, and as roosters do, he would loudly crow several times a day—a sound we knew would attract the bobcat.

The cat only came in that area once a week, but we checked the trap every day. The first morning after we set the trap, sure enough the green opossum was in there! He wanted that rooster, but he couldn't figure out how to get to it!

My friend was not discouraged. He looked at me and said, "Let me show you how to outsmart this guy." He released the opossum and tied the door open so that the opossum could come and go as he pleased. Mark explained that the opossum would lose interest in the rooster eventually and leave the area once he figured out he couldn't eat it.

The bobcat wouldn't be back for a week, so we came back to check the trap about five days later. To our surprise, the trap door was still tied wide open, but there was that stupid green opossum! He was sitting there dead with a smile on his face, looking straight up at the rooster! He was determined to eat that rooster—and had literally starved to death trying to do it. He was too focused and too dumb to turn around and walk out of the open door of that trap. The opossum never realized he could leave anytime because he was too fascinated by the bait!

Horse-Sense Interpretation

Don't let your desires keep you in a trap when the doorway of escape is open. Turn around and leave! You must forsake what you think you really want (drugs, money, etc.) in order to get what God says you need.

Lust destroys a person, just like that opossum's stubborn desires ended its life. I've met people through my involvement in a jail ministry who say they hunger for God, but in the end they wanted their sin even more. The wrong desires in life can get a hold on us that will hurt us. People aren't *hooked* on drugs—they're *choosing* that lifestyle. You can make a different choice.

If you come to Christ, He can change your desires and give you knew, fresh, clean, and wholesome desires. Our worldly desires are not as important as doing what God needs us to do.

Trapping is not a money-making profession, and I was often short of money. Still, I used to buy a lottery ticket every week for $5.00 for about ten years. Every week! I told God all about how I would use the money for Him if He would only let me win. But one day I realized I was cheating God out of money that rightfully belonged to Him. I stopped going into the gas station for my usual Dr. Pepper and a lottery ticket! My desires changed overnight.

When I was a young man, I was once on a path to becoming a world champion rodeo star. I said that I wanted it for God's sake, but I really wanted the glory for myself deep in my heart. At 28 years of old, I had to give up my heart's desire to become a champion, and I became a servant instead. God put me on a brand-new path instead. I had to leave what I thought was a good thing behind in order to pursue God's best for me. And I am glad I did!

> *As a dog returneth to his vomit, so a fool returneth to his folly.*
> **Proverbs 26:11**

> *Turn you at my reproof; behold I will pour out my spirit unto you; I will make known my words unto you.*
> **Proverbs 1:23**

Forsake the foolish, and live; and go in the way of understanding.

Proverbs 9:6

I tell you, Nay: but except ye repent, ye shall all likewise perish.

Luke 13:3

Made in the USA
Columbia, SC
23 January 2023

10307664R00072